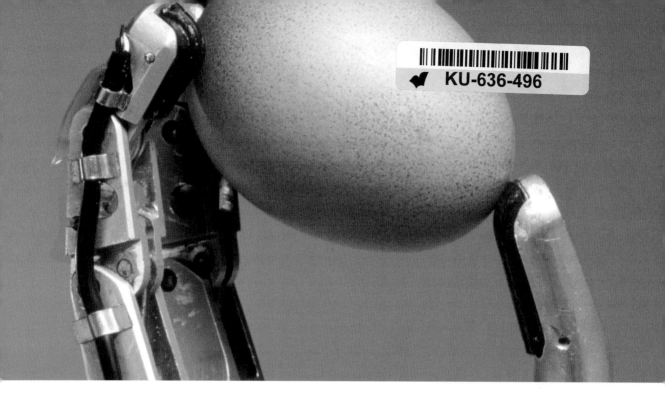

CUTTING EDGE MEDICINE

Machines in Medicine

Anne Rooney

FRANKLIN WATTS
LONDON • SYDNEY

First published in 2007 by
Franklin Watts
338 Euston Road
London NW1 3BH

Franklin Watts Australia
Hachette Children's Books
Level 17/207 Kent St, Sydney, NSW 2000

Produced by Arcturus Publishing Limited
26/27 Bickels Yard, 151–153 Bermondsey Street
London SE1 3HA

The right of Anne Rooney to be identified as the author of this work has been asserted by her in accordance with the Copyright, Designs and Patents Act, 1988.
www.annerooney.co.uk

Editor: Alex Woolf
Designer: Nick Phipps
Consultant: Dr Eleanor Clarke

Picture credits:
Science Photo Library: 4 (CC Studio), 7 (Sheila Terry), 8 (Geoff Tompkinson), 10 (Damien Lovegrove), 12 (Tracy Dominey), 14 (Steve Allen), 16 (Jim Varney), 19 (Maximilianstock Ltd), 20 (Gusto), 23 (Samuel Ashfield), 25 (Malcolm Fielding, the BOC Group plc), 27 (AJ Photo), 28 (Stanley B. Burns, MD, and the Burns Archive, N.Y.), 30 (Eye of Science), 32 (Pascal Goetgheluck), 34 (Peter Menzel), 36 (Deep Light Productions), 39 (Du Cane Medical Imaging Ltd), 40 (Antonia Reeve), 43 (Hank Morgan), 44 (BSIP Laurent/H Americain), 46 (SIU), 49 (Sovereign, ISM), 51 (James King-Holmes), 52 (Volker Steger, Peter Arnold Inc.), 55 (Hattie Young), 56 (Mauro Fermariello), 58 (Christian Darkin).

Every attempt has been made to clear copyright. Should there be any inadvertent omission, please apply to the publisher for rectification.

A CIP catalogue record for this book is available from the British Library.

Dewey Decimal Classification Number: 618.1'780599

ISBN: 978 0 7496 6971 3

Printed in China

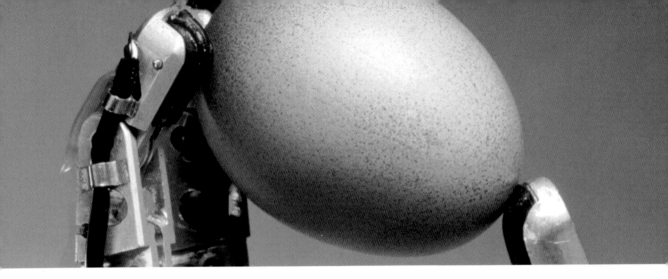

Contents

CHAPTER 1

What's the Problem?

A person who falls ill in the 21st century stands a much better chance of survival and full recovery than someone who fell ill a hundred or even fifty years ago. Improved understanding of the human body and how it works has enabled doctors to diagnose and treat illness more effectively. Alongside this knowledge, many tools, instruments and other items of medical equipment have been developed and refined that help medical staff at all stages of care. Tools range from simple items, such as thermometers, to very sophisticated machinery controlled by computers and tiny instruments manipulated under a microscope.

Although simple, the stethoscope is an invaluable tool for listening to body sounds.

As increasingly complicated equipment becomes available, medical staff can identify and treat problems more quickly and in different ways. Many people owe their lives to machines used in medicine, and many more depend on them to live normal, full lives.

A doctor's expertise

Doctors train for many years and are experts at diagnosis (working out what is wrong with someone). An important part of diagnosis is talking to patients, asking about how they feel and getting them to describe how their problem has developed. But not all patients can talk to a doctor. Babies and young children, or people who are unconscious or in severe pain or distress, cannot answer questions. In such cases, the doctor must examine the patient, looking for symptoms (signs of illness or injury). Tools and equipment can reveal symptoms that the doctor cannot see alone and that even the patient may not be able to identify.

Simple machines

A doctor will often check a patient's temperature, listen to his or her heart and lungs, and perhaps look into the patient's eyes, ears and mouth. These simple tests use equipment that has been around for centuries – but sometimes, with the expertise of a doctor or healthworker, they are enough to show what is wrong.

CUTTING EDGE MOMENTS

Important early medical inventions

Who	What
René-Théophile-Hyacinthe Laënnec (1781–1826)	Invented the first stethoscope in 1816. It was a wooden cylinder 30 cm long.
Hermann von Helmholtz (1821–1894)	Invented the ophthalmoscope in 1850, allowing doctors to see the living retina for the first time.
John Brunton (1836–1899)	Invented the otoscope in 1862
Sir Thomas Clifford Allbutt (1836–1925)	Invented the clinical thermometer in 1866, allowing a patient's temperature to be measured in a few minutes. Previously it had taken more than 20 minutes to measure temperatures with an instrument 30 cm long.
Samuel Siegfried Karl Ritter von Basch (1837–1905)	Invented the first sphygmomanometer in 1881. It consisted of a water-filled bag connected to a manometer (pressure meter).
Scipione Riva-Rocci (1863–1937)	Developed the mercury sphygmomanometer – the basis of the modern device – in 1896.

Thermometer A classical thermometer, used to measure body temperature, is a glass tube with a column of expanding liquid inside and a scale marked up the side, though today a doctor will use a digital thermometer. Thermometers are used to diagnose an unusually high or low temperature. High temperature is an indication of fever, a symptom of many illnesses.

Otoscope An otoscope is used to look inside the ear. It has a light and a magnifying lens in the tip, which is put just inside the outer ear. The doctor looks through the lens to see the inside of the ear canal and ear drum. Using it, the doctor may be able to see if the ear is infected, damaged or blocked.

Sphygmomanometer A sphygmomanometer is used to measure blood pressure. A rubber cuff is fitted tightly around the arm while a doctor or nurse pumps air into it and listens with a stethoscope, reading the blood pressure from a dial. A sphygmomanometer is used to detect unusually high or low blood pressure. High blood pressure is common in people with blocked blood vessels or with heart conditions.

Stethoscope A stethoscope is used to magnify sounds from the heart, lungs and other organs. It has a cup at one end, which the doctor presses against the body, and tubes leading to earpieces. It is used to diagnose abnormal heart or lung function. An irregular heartbeat, or laboured breathing, can be detected with a stethoscope.

CUTTING EDGE   SCIENCE

Ultrasound stethoscopes

Ultrasound is produced by a crystal, similar to that in a quartz watch, vibrating about two million times a second. The high-frequency sound waves travel through liquid but are reflected back from solid bodies, producing an echo that is picked up by a detector in the stethoscope. It can measure the sounds reflected back from moving blood cells under layers of fat in an obese patient, or pick up the heartbeat of an unborn child inside its mother.

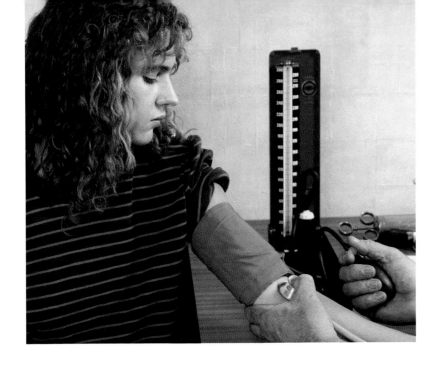

A doctor measures a patient's blood pressure using a stethoscope and a sphygmomanometer.

Ophthalmoscope An ophthalmoscope has a light and a magnifying lens for looking into the eye. The light bounces off the back of the eye (the retina), illuminating it for the doctor or ophthalmologist (an eye specialist). The opthalmoscope can show up problems in the eye and also reveal pressure in the blood vessels or brain – conditions that are not local to the eye, but are revealed in the appearance of the vessels in the retina.

Getting better all the time

Even the simplest of tools have been greatly improved by modern technology, increasing precision and reducing the possibility of human error.

Since the 1990s, accurate and sensitive digital thermometers have been in common use. They give a precise reading of body temperature in seconds.

Sophisticated stethoscopes that work with ultrasound (high-pitched sounds) can measure the flow of blood in blood vessels deep inside the body and help to assess the condition of the heart. They can reveal narrowed or blocked arteries or veins that hinder blood flow and lead to serious problems, such as stroke.

Digital sphygmomanometers show a read-out of blood pressure on a screen, indicate if the cuff is not properly placed on the arm, and inflate and deflate the cuff automatically.

Newer otoscopes combine fibre optic light and a digital screen and can make a range of tones to help test hearing.

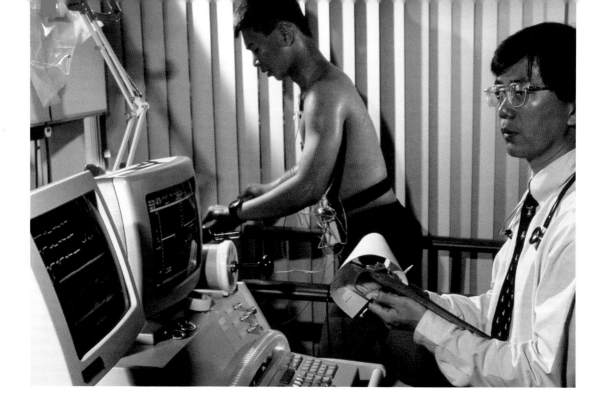

Electric bodies

The human body creates tiny pulses of electricity that carry messages around the nervous system, the network of nerves and nerve cells that enables us to sense the outside world and to control our muscles. Instruments that can pick up these electrical pulses are used to monitor conditions in the body and diagnose problems.

Electrocardiograph An electrocardiograph (ECG) measures the electric pulses in the muscles of the heart. Electrodes (pads or wires that pick up electric current) are fastened to the patient's body, usually on the chest and hands, and detect electric current from the heart. The ECG produces a graph called an electrocardiogram. If a patient has a healthy heart, the graph will show regular peaks as the muscles of the heart expand and contract. An irregular heartbeat, abnormally sized chambers of the heart, and some blood pressure problems can be diagnosed from an unusual electrocardiogram.

Electroencephalograph An electroencephalograph (EEG), measures brain activity using pairs of electrodes placed on the scalp. The brain is packed with nerve cells and produces lots of electrical activity. An EEG, which produces a graph similar to an ECG, can help to diagnose brain tumours, epilepsy, injuries, infections of the brain and some diseases that affect the nerves.

An electrocardiograph machine monitors a patient's heartbeat through electrodes attached to his chest, while he exercises.

Electromyelograph An electromyelograph (EMG) measures electrical pulses in the muscles. It is used to check muscle activity and the action of the nerves controlling the muscles. EMG can help diagnose the causes of muscle weakness, revealing whether it is caused by disorders of the nerves, such as carpal tunnel syndrome, or deterioration of the muscles themselves, such as muscular dystrophy. A thin electrode, like a hypodermic needle, is pushed through the skin into the muscle and attached to an oscilloscope, a device for measuring electric current. When the patient uses the muscle - bending an arm or leg, for instance - the current is measured, producing a similar graph to an ECG or an EEG.

Portable tests

Small, portable EEG and ECG equipment allows doctors and paramedics to diagnose some problems at the scene of an emergency. This is particularly useful for spotting heart attacks and stroke, which must be treated immediately. Some machines can transmit data directly from the equipment to a distant receiver.

CUTTING EDGE MOMENTS

Measuring the body's electricity

1884	John Burden Sanderson and Frederick Page (UK) record the heart's electrical current, showing it has two phases.
1887	Augustus Waller (UK) makes the first electrocardiogram.
1895	Willem Einthoven (the Netherlands) identifies five different phases of electrical current shown in a electrocardiogram.
1905	Willem Einthoven transmits electrocardiograms 1.5 km from the hospital to his laboratory using the telephone cables.
1924	Hans Berger (Germany) produces the first electroencephalograms.
1928	Frank Sanborn's company (USA) produces the first portable ECG.
2005	In Denmark, data from an ECG in an ambulance is transmitted by wireless network to the PDA (Personal Digital Assistant) of a cardiologist at a hospital, who can make a remote diagnosis.

Breathing

Medical machinery can help diagnose and treat lung problems for people with breathing disorders, such as asthma. One of the first tasks in diagnosing breathing difficulties is to measure the lung capacity, often using a device called a peak flow meter. A peak flow

A peak flow meter is a simple way of measuring lung function. Many patients use them at home to monitor the condition of their lungs.

meter consists of a plastic tube and a slider that moves along a numbered scale showing the volume of air exhaled (breathed out). It measures the amount of air a person can breathe in and blow out. This amount is called the forced vital capacity of the lungs. If the volume of air is less than 80 per cent of the average for a person of that size and age, the patient may need treatment to improve his or her lung function.

The digital spirometer is a more sophisticated tool for measuring lung function. It also measures the forced vital capacity of a patient's lungs, but the technology is more refined and accurate. The volume and force of the patient's exhalation is measured by an electronic sensor and can be compared with other data stored in the spirometer, or on a computer, to track the patient's progress or compare the reading with expected or average levels. Using a digital spirometer, a doctor can work out the patient's lung capacity, the rate at which air flows through the lungs, and the tidal volume – the amount of air breathed in and out when the patient breathes normally. The measurements can show up obstructions or restrictions in the lungs and airways.

CUTTING EDGE   SCIENTISTS

Basil Martin Wright

Basil Wright (1912–2001) was a bioengineer with a flare for invention. In 1949, he joined the Medical Research Council's unit for pneumoconiosis (a lung disease caused by inhaling mineral or metallic dust). He found that the unit, based at Llandough in Wales, UK, lacked the equipment needed to undertake large-scale studies of lung capacity. To remedy the situation, he invented the first peak flow meter in 1959. This made studies of lung function possible, and so led to a greater understanding of lung disease. The first peak flow meters were large and cumbersome, but Wright designed a personal, portable model in 1974. Many people with asthma use these at home to monitor their lung function. Wright moved to the National Institute for Medical Research (London) in 1957 and concentrated solely on developing new instruments. He invented a device called a respirometer, which is still used to give anaesthetics (pain-relieving drugs) to patients during surgery and to administer continuous pain relief to dying patients. The roadside breathalyser used by the police to test drivers' breath for alcohol is based on Wright's respirometer.

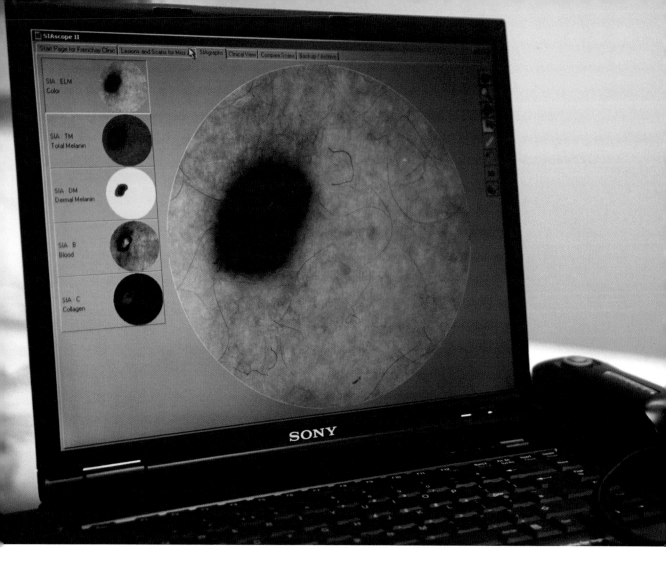

Computers in diagnosis

Until fairly recently, doctors had to depend on their own knowledge and on reference charts and books to diagnose and treat a patient's condition. These are still invaluable, and the expertise and intuition of doctors can never be replaced by technology, but computers are taking on an increasingly important role, too.

A medical expert system is a computer application that brings together the knowledge of many experts. It can provide a comprehensive resource that can be shared by doctors everywhere and can take some of the work out of diagnosis. Expert systems draw upon extensive records and information about a wide range of diseases and disorders, and can search and analyse all this information in moments.

By putting together the results of all the tests that a doctor or hospital has run on a patient, an expert system can make intelligent

A computer is used with a portable device called a SIAscope to aid diagnosis of skin lesions, such as this mole shown in a magnified view on the screen.

diagnoses or suggestions. This saves time, as the comparison and analysis is almost instantaneous. It also draws on more expertise than a single doctor or specialist is ever likely to have. Expert systems are especially good for spotting unusual conditions that a doctor may not think of or even have come across before. But a human doctor usually fares better than a computer if the patient's symptoms are the result of two or more conditions. This is because a computer first looks for a condition that combines all the symptoms, whereas a doctor may recognize groups of symptoms that lead him or her to suspect there is more than one condition affecting the patient.

In hospitals, computers can be used with various types of scanners to produce three-dimensional images of the inside of the body, often vital in spotting problems and directing surgery. After human experts have confirmed a diagnosis, the computer can help again by presenting possibilities for treatment and modelling outcomes and risks for different treatments.

Asking questions

Patients can even diagnose their own conditions in some cases by using an online computer database. The patient fills in a questionnaire on a screen, and the computer will attempt to diagnose the problem. Sometimes, patients may be able to avoid a visit to the surgery completely if they are able to diagnose a simple condition that is not dangerous.

CUTTING EDGE   SCIENCE

Fuzzy logic and diagnostics
Expert systems use a technique called 'fuzzy logic'. This works on approximations and probabilities rather than absolute numbers. Instead of trying to match symptoms precisely to illnesses, fuzzy logic assesses how well symptoms match expected symptoms for different illnesses, allowing degrees of variation. This is a more reliable basis for medical diagnosis since the appearance of symptoms in different patients is likely to vary. Strict rules for diagnosing a patient's condition could lead to a large number of misdiagnoses because possible disorders would be excluded too readily.

CHAPTER 2

In the Medical Lab

A visit to the doctor or clinic is often just the first stage of diagnosis. There may be much work to do behind the scenes, examining and analysing samples taken from the patient. These can include tests on blood or other body fluids, and on biopsies (small pieces of tissue removed either by surgery or with a needle). The tests look for abnormal patterns of growth, abnormally shaped cells and bacteria (micro-organisms that can cause disease).

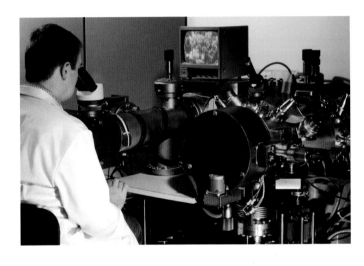

A researcher uses a scanning electron microscope to examine blood cells in the laboratory.

Microscopes

Microscopes provide a magnified view of items too small to see with the naked eye. Simple microscopes use only one lens, while compound microscopes use several. Many microscopes have a single eyepiece; some, called binocular microscopes, have two eyepieces so that the user can use both eyes. Some microscopes are connected to computers and can project the magnified image onto a screen, make measurements and carry out comparisons and calculations on them. For example, using a microscope, a doctor can compare healthy cells and diseased cells that may be cancerous. A cell from the human body may be only 10 microns across. (A micron is one thousandth of a millimetre, or one twenty-five-thousandths of an inch) A microscope connected to a computer can store images from different samples and bring them up for comparison side by side so that the doctor can see whether there are significant differences between them.

Preparing samples

Microscopes can be used to look at samples of a liquid or solid. Either may be dyed with a stain so that particular structures or materials show up clearly in colour. For example, bacteria causing an infection may be revealed in a stained smear sample. Samples are usually held on a slide (a thin plate of glass) and covered with a glass cover.

Some samples are also treated with a chemical called a fixative, which stops changes taking place in the sample. Samples from a body can contain many enzymes and micro-organisms that will break down the tissues and make the sample less useful. Fixing the sample stops this process, 'freezing' it in the state that it was in when taken from the body.

Solid samples are treated with and set in paraffin wax and cut into thin slices so that light can shine through them. Samples of a solid organ such as the liver are too dense to examine unless very thinly sliced. The wax holds the sample firm so that the tissue is not squashed and distorted by cutting.

CUTTING EDGE   SCIENCE

Microscopes

Modern microscopes range from small optical (light) microscopes to large and powerful scanning and transmission electron microscopes. An optical microscope uses lenses to magnify the image by bending rays of light. The level of magnification is limited by the wavelength of light, which eventually causes the image to distort.

An electron microscope uses magnetic lenses to move beams of electrons (very tiny components of the atoms that make up all matter). The wavelength of a beam of electrons is much smaller than that of light, so accurate, clear images can be achieved at greater magnifications. There are two types of electron microscope. A scanning electron microscope (SEM) is used for looking at the surface of objects. A transmission electron microscope (TEM) fires electrons straight through a sample. It gives a higher resolution image (showing more detail) and can give information about the internal structure of the sample.

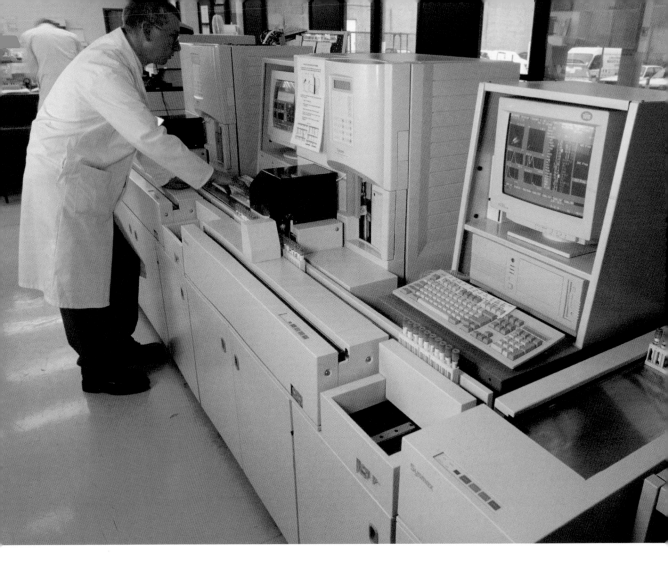

Picking out problems

After receiving a sample from a patient, laboratory staff pick out the parts they want to look at, either isolating them from the sample or identifying them under the microscope. Sometimes, solids are extracted from a liquid sample by centrifuging (spinning at high speed) or filtering the liquid.

Researchers can stain or dye a sample to show the cellular features that they need to see. The dye makes different cell structures clear, and the amount of dye that is absorbed shows the different densities or compositions of material in the sample. Dyes can reveal harmful micro-organisms such as bacteria, and abnormalities in or damage to body tissue or cells. Some bacteria, known as Gram-positive because they absorb a purple dye called Gram, look purple or blue. Others don't retain the dye well and look pink. These are Gram-negative bacteria. Using the Gram dye can

A technician analyses blood using a Coulter counter.

therefore help narrow the possibilities when diagnosing a bacterial infection.

Sometimes, a special type of dye is injected into tissue before a sample is taken. Radioactive dyes – dyes that emit a small amount of radioactivity (beams of energy) – may be injected near a cancerous growth, for example. A surgeon can then detect the radioactive areas and take a biopsy sample from them. By using dyes known to bind to particular cancer cells, the surgeon can ensure that exactly the right cells are removed for examination.

Counters and analyzers

Many samples are taken with the aim of counting or identifying cells or features of a certain type. In a blood sample, for instance, the investigation may include a blood count – a count of how many red and white blood cells are present. For example, allergies and the disease leukaemia lead to unusually high numbers of certain types of white blood cells; too few red blood cells is a symptom of a condition called anaemia. During fertility treatment, a man may be asked to give a sample of semen for a sperm count. If there are fewer than the normal number of sperm, the man may experience low fertility. These counts are carried out automatically by a computerized device called a semen analyzer.

CUTTING EDGE   SCIENCE

Laser tweezers
Sometimes it is necessary to separate different types of cells – sorting healthy ones from diseased ones, for example. Individual cells and parts of cells can be picked out or moved around using laser or optical tweezers. These use beams of light to move cells or parts of cells without damaging them. Laser beams are moved rapidly by a system of moving mirrors, or spread into intricate patterns. A pattern of interconnecting laser beams acts like a trap or a mesh of light, letting through only particles smaller than the mesh. Moving laser beams can also be used to nudge particles into position. This technique can be used to move tiny strands of DNA into a cell during research into and treatment of inherited diseases. The most advanced laser tweezers can also be used for spectroscopy – measuring how the particles scatter the laser light reveals their shape, sizes and chemical composition.

Profilers

Complex systems incorporating several machines can provide a complete profile of a sample when multiple tests are needed. These make various measurements and analyses and combine the results to give a full picture. For example, profiling a blood sample will give a complete blood count (counts of the different types of blood cells) and also information about the levels of chemicals, hormones (natural 'messenger' chemicals released into the bloodstream), nutrients and any contaminants (chemicals that should not be present) in the blood.

DNA profiling is a way of finding out about a patient's genetic make-up. DNA is the material from which genes and chromosomes are made. Every person has a unique genetic make-up, and a complete DNA profile is a map of this. A profile can be used to match a sample with an individual – identifying the victim of an accident, for example. Or it can be used to pinpoint specific features, such as identifying a hereditary disease or disorder. DNA profiling can be used to test embryos (unborn babies in the early stage of their development) produced during in vitro fertilization (embryos created in the laboratory from egg and sperm cells) to exclude any with an inherited disorder. Any embryos found to have an inherited disorder will be rejected and not implanted.

CUTTING EDGE   **SCIENCE**

Spotting cells

Samples of body tissue taken for cancer testing are usually examined under a microscope by a cytologist – an expert in cells. This is a time-consuming process, prone to human error. Computer image-matching systems are replacing some screening by humans in the detection of cervical cancer from smear tests. The computer takes images from a camera and microscope and compares them with images of the nuclei (centres) of normal and cancerous cells. Where a cell appears to match a cancerous type, it is flagged as suspect.

Chemical tests

Other complex chemical procedures are often used with liquid samples such as blood, urine and other body fluids.

Mass spectrometry measures the mass of molecules and is a way of working out the chemical composition of a sample. It can be used in blood samples to spot performance-enhancing drugs taken by athletes, for instance.

A scientist examines a test tube of liquid separated from a sample using chromatography.

Chromatography is a method of separating and identifying the constituents of a liquid or gas. The sample is mixed with a carrier, either as a liquid or gas, and moves over a stationary bed of an absorbent material. Different components are absorbed at different rates or travel further through the column of absorbent material. Technicians read the results as a line graph consisting of a series of peaks. The position of the peaks and the area under them indicate the concentrations of different constituents.

Gel electrophoresis uses an electrical charge to separate molecules (tiny particles that are the smallest component of a substance) of different sizes in a sample set in gel. Charged particles move towards or away from a source of electricity. The speed of their movement reveals their size, as the largest molecules move most slowly. Technicians read the results as a series of shaded strips. The amount of shading indicates the percentages of the different constituents.

CHAPTER 3

Emergency!

Not all medical investigations take an ordered course. Often, medical staff must deal with emergency situations, such as accidents, where every second counts. The patient's survival or full recovery may depend on the care he or she receives in the first few critical minutes, and medical machinery can be a lifesaver.

Breathing problems

Sudden breathing difficulties can be very dangerous. The brain needs oxygen all the time to function, and if disturbances to breathing limit the amount of oxygen carried in the blood, brain damage and death can happen alarmingly quickly. People may suffer breathing difficulties for many reasons, but one of the most common is a sudden asthma attack. This is often treated using a

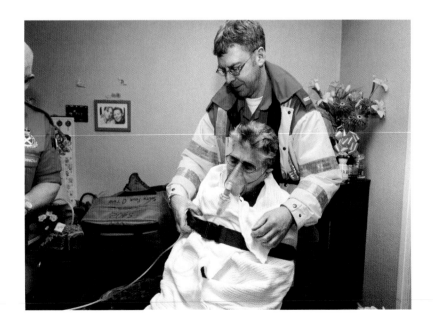

A paramedic assists an elderly patient suffering from breathing difficulties. Prompt action is vital in emergencies involving lung function.

machine called a nebulizer, which produces a very fine aerosol (spray) of medicine suspended as tiny droplets in the air. The nebulizer delivers the medicine through the patient's nose and mouth to the lungs, where it acts to relax the muscles and open the constricted airways.

Sometimes, patients need extra oxygen quickly. This can happen if they have been exposed to smoke or poisonous gases, or if extra oxygen is needed to help healing, to combat disease or to treat a breathing problem. The oxygen is usually supplied through a mask that covers the patient's nose and mouth.

Occasionally, oxygen is supplied at high pressure to increase the rate at which the blood can take up and carry oxygen to tissues that need it. It is used sometimes for wounds that will not heal, to treat divers with decompression sickness (caused by surfacing from a dive too quickly), for some types of radiation sickness and for carbon monoxide poisoning (common in people who have been involved in house fires). The oxygen is given to the patient in a special high-pressure chamber so that the extra pressure outside the body forces the oxygen into the patient quickly. This is called hyperbaric oxygen therapy (see panel).

CUTTING EDGE   SCIENCE

Hyperbaric oxygen therapy (HBOT)

Hyperbaric oxygen therapy involves giving patients oxygen at up to double normal atmospheric pressure. Patients are commonly treated in a large metal chamber that can hold several people at once. Each patient wears a transparent plastic hood that delivers the oxygen. They are attended by a specially trained nurse. Patients can stand, sit or lie down and may be able to watch videos, read or sleep while receiving the treatment.

New capillaries (very tiny blood vessels) form quickly in wounded areas as a response to the extra oxygen, aiding healing. When breathed in under pressure, the oxygen is transmitted two to three times as far into the tissues from the capillaries, so damaged areas can quickly gain enough oxygen to heal. The oxygen also improves the ability of the white blood cells to destroy some types of harmful bacteria by a factor of two to three.

Heart and blood

Among the most common emergencies involving the heart and the circulatory system (the system of blood vessels) are heart attack and stroke. In a heart attack, an artery (a blood vessel carrying oxygenated blood) in the heart becomes blocked and part of the heart muscle stops functioning. Within three to four minutes of a heart attack, the heart stops beating and must be restarted very quickly if the patient is to survive. In a stroke, the blood supply to the brain is interrupted, usually because a blood clot (a lump of solidifying blood) blocks one of the arteries.

A paramedic with a portable ECG (see pages 8 and 9) can confirm the diagnosis of heart attack, measure the functioning of the heart and determine the severity of the damage caused by the heart attack. If the heart stops beating properly, it can be restarted with a defibrillator. This uses pairs of pads containing electrodes that, when attached to the patient's chest, pass an electric shock to the heart to jolt it into beating regularly.

The early defibrillators were about the size and weight of a car battery, and not easily moved. The first portable model was designed by the physician and cardiologist Frank Pantridge, from County Down, Northern Ireland. He also developed the idea of providing coronary care in ambulances. Many ambulances now carry defibrillators. Planes and some public buildings also have

CUTTING EDGE   SCIENTISTS

Mieczyslaw Mirowski

Mieczyslaw Mirowski (1924–1990) was born in Warsaw, Poland. At different periods of his life he lived in Poland, Israel, France (where he trained in medicine), Mexico and the USA. While he was in Israel, the death of a close colleague from heart disease in 1966 inspired him to develop a ventricular defibrillator that could be implanted directly into the heart. This would be capable of restarting a person's heart if it stopped. The medical profession did not support Mirowski's plan, which was considered unworkable, and he had to fight hostility and lack of funding before successfully completing a prototype in 1975. After testing on dogs, the first AID (automatic implantable defibrillator) was implanted in a human patient in 1980. Over the next five years, 800 patients received an AID.

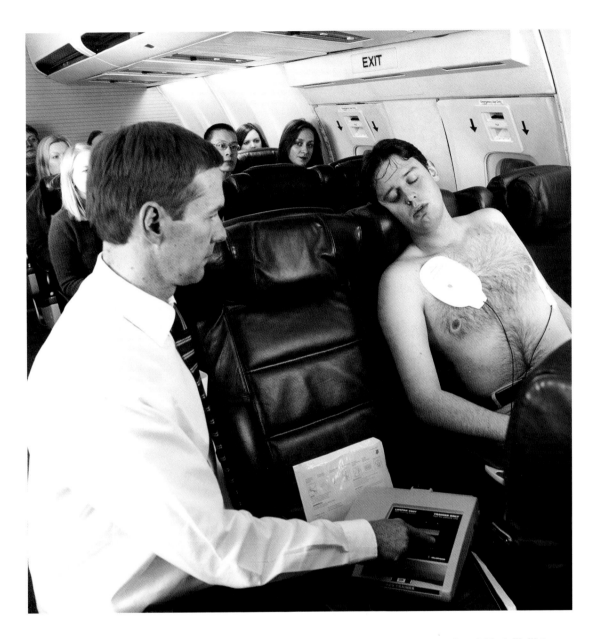

portable defibrillators so that heart attack patients can be treated immediately, avoiding a delay that could be fatal.

A portable defibrillator on an airliner is used to treat a patient who has suffered a cardiac arrest during a flight.

Bleeding

If a person loses a lot of blood, they can die quite quickly. The best way to prevent blood loss after a serious injury is to clamp the severed blood vessel using a simple tool called a haemostatic clamp, or haemostat. This looks like a pair of scissors, but with a locking clamp in place of blades.

Since the late 1980s, a substance called microfibrillar collagen haemostat is often applied to wounds in place of mechanical clamps. This substance contains artificial collagen; collagen is the protein that forms the connective tissue that supports and binds together other tissue such as muscle, blood vessels and skin. The haemostat attracts platelets (a type of blood cell), which clump together and form a natural clot, stopping the bleeding.

Intensive care

When a person is very ill or badly injured, they may need several different kinds of care to treat more than one body system at the same time. Modern hospitals are equipped with intensive care units that have a range of complex machinery to monitor body functions and provide constant and immediate care. These machines can keep a patient alive who would die without this level of care – for example, people suffering from extreme breathing problems, kidney failure, multi-organ failure and sepsis (blood poisoning). The first intensive care unit was established in Copenhagen, Denmark, in 1953 by Bjorn Ibsen in response to a polio epidemic, which left many victims with severe breathing difficulties requiring artificial ventilation.

Patients in intensive care are connected to monitors that track vital signs such as their heart rate, blood pressure, temperature, breathing and the levels of oxygen and carbon dioxide in their blood. Computers combine the data from the different monitors to

CUTTING EDGE   DEBATES

Turning off the machine

Patients can often be kept alive by machinery in an intensive care unit, on a life support system, long beyond the point when they would have died without such advanced care. Some patients can be sustained indefinitely, though they have no chance of recovering and living a normal life. If a patient has no chance of recovery, medical staff may suggest that the artificial ventilators are turned off, or that feeding through tubes is withdrawn, and the patient is allowed to die. It is a contentious issue, and when there are disagreements between medical staff and family members, the courts may be called on to decide whether the patient should remain on life support or die.

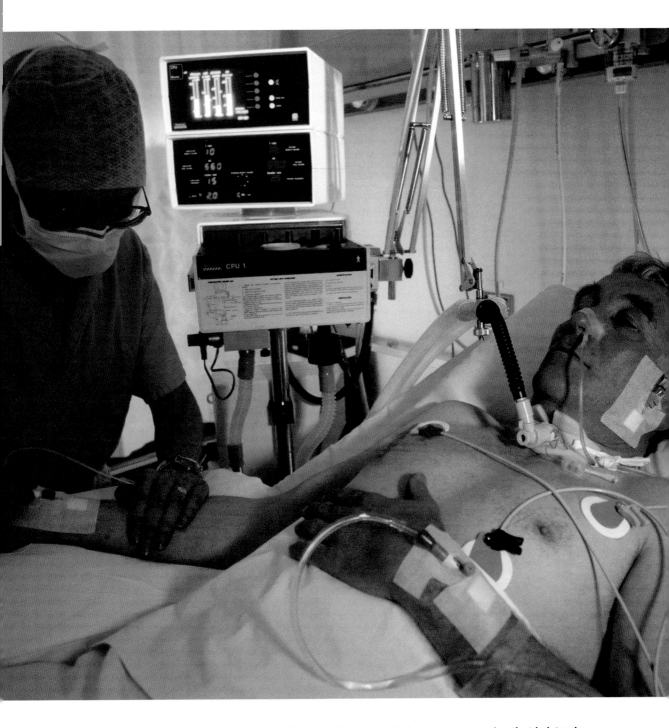

provide a real-time, complete report of the patient's vital signs at a glance. Display screens and warning systems in the intensive care unit immediately alert the medical staff to any changes in the patient's condition.

A patient in intensive care is constantly monitored and receives treatments from an array of machinery.

Some people in intensive care need help with breathing or with the function of organs such as the kidneys. A ventilator takes over the task of breathing for the patient. A ventilator is a machine that pumps the right amount of air into the lungs, mimicking the person's normal breathing.

Neonatal care

Very tiny babies need specialized care and specially adapted medical equipment. Newborn and pre-term babies (those born before they have spent nine months in the womb) have delicate and finely balanced systems. Pre-term babies have not finished their development and often need assistance with breathing while they continue to grow.

Very ill newborn babies and pre-term babies are cared for in a special neonatal intensive care unit. In the unit, all babies lie in incubators. These provide a temperature-controlled environment that keeps the baby warm. Respiratory distress syndrome, which causes difficulty in breathing, is particularly common in pre-term babies. These babies need ventilators to help them breathe. Many babies in neonatal intensive care are fed through tubes that go through the nose and down the throat into the stomach, as they have not developed sufficiently to suck milk from a bottle or breast.

CUTTING EDGE   FACTS

Oxygen and infant blindness

The development of incubators that could provide an oxygen-rich environment for small babies brought an unexpected problem in the form of retrolental fibroplasias (RLF), a disease that causes blindness by narrowing the arteries in the retina. Doctors noticed the high incidence of RLF in preterm babies in the 1940s, caused by exposure to high concentrations of oxygen in incubators. Yet withholding the oxygen could cause brain damage or death. In the 1950s, they solved the problem by restricting babies' exposure to high levels of oxygen. All babies are now very carefully monitored to make sure they are not suffering damage as a result of too much or too little oxygen, and the incidence of RLF is greatly reduced.

As neonatal intensive care is a specialized branch of medicine requiring expensive high-tech equipment, some larger hospitals handle it for a wide geographic area. Specially equipped neonatal ambulances are used to move sick babies to and between neonatal care units. These have incubators and ventilators on board, so that the baby's care can continue during the journey.

A pre-term baby is cared for in an incubator in a neonatal unit.

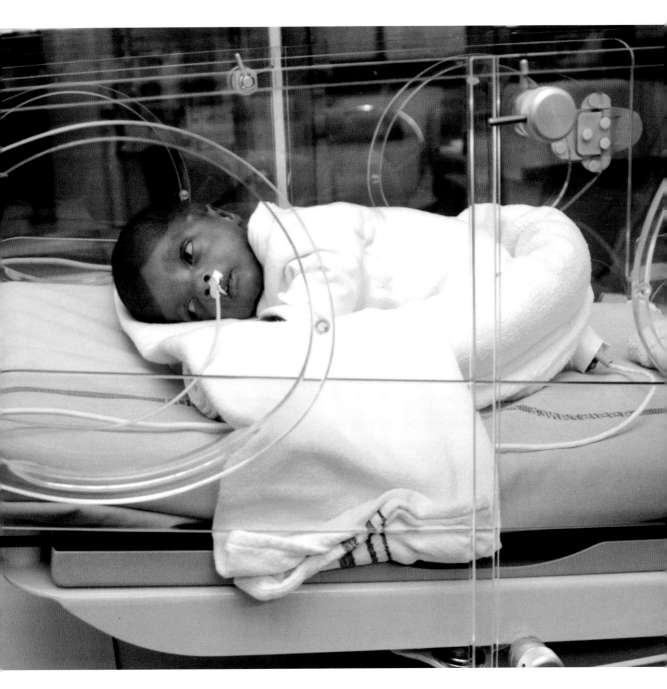

CHAPTER 4

Surgery and Operations

The simplest surgical tools such as knives and forceps have been in use for thousands of years. Arab surgeons developed instruments as long ago as the ninth century CE that are similar to many still in use today. But modern surgeons can draw on an array of machines to help them in their work. Some machines help keep patients stable and anaesthetized (unconscious and free of pain) during operations, while other machines assist the surgeon in the operation or surgical procedure.

Controlling pain

An anaesthetic prevents the patient from feeling pain. In the days before anaesthetics were available, surgery could be brutal and

The advent of anaesthesia finally made operations like this leg amputation in 1857 bearable for the patient and easier for the surgeon.

Delivering anaesthetic gases

An anaesthesia machine mixes a vaporized anaesthetic with a supply of gases, usually oxygen and nitrogen, and delivers the mix to the patient through a mask or tube. The nitrogen and oxygen are generally piped through the hospital. Supply tubes from the wall are plugged into the machine, which has back-up cylinders of gas in case the central supply fails. The machine has one or more vaporizers, which feed carefully measured small quantities of anaesthetic vapour into the flow of gases delivered to the patient. Flow meters and pressure gauges are used to monitor and control the flow so that the patient is not exposed to high pressures. Anaesthetic gas is removed from the air breathed out by the patient and discharged outside the room. Monitors, alarms and safety systems make sure the patient cannot receive too much or too little of any of the constituents and alert staff if the equipment fails in any way. Vital signs are monitored with electronic sensors at all times.

painful for the patient. Patients often had to be held down by assistants and were sometimes given something, such as a stick, to bite on. The surgeon's work was limited by how long the patient could be kept still and endure the pain of surgery. Great progress has been made in surgery since anaesthetics have become available.

General anaesthetics render patients unconscious: they are unaware of anything happening to them and feel no pain. A local anaesthetic works on just one part of the body, making it numb. Whenever possible, surgeons prefer to use a local anaesthetic. It causes less stress and disruption to the body and allows the patient to remain communicative. Many local anaesthetics are given in the form of an injection of a natural or artificial alkaloid (a type of nitrogen-containing chemical found in plants), such as Novocaine, that numbs the area to be treated.

Block anaesthetics are injected near a major nerve to deaden a large area. The best known is the spinal block or epidural anaesthetic often given to women during childbirth. This prevents pain messages from being passed up the spinal cord to the brain, so the patient is not aware of any discomfort. A thin tube is connected to a needle inserted into the spine and the anaesthetic is delivered steadily through the tube. Local anaesthetics have no lasting effects or side effects and wear off quickly without affecting other parts of the body.

General anaesthetics may be given by injection or as a gas, which the patient breathes in using a mask that fits over the face; a pipe may be passed down the throat into the lungs after the patient is

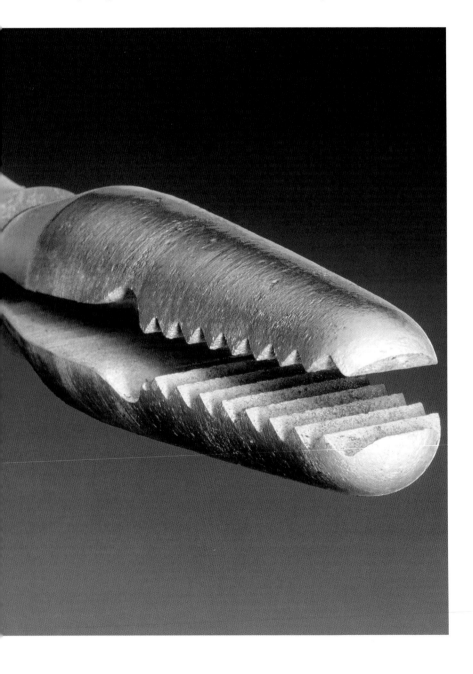

A photograph taken through a microscope of a clamp used in microsurgery on the brain. The clamp is only 0.63 mm in diameter.

asleep. A qualified anaesthetist uses computerized equipment to monitor the patient's breathing, heart rate, blood pressure and the level of oxygen in the blood. If there is any change in these vital signs, the level of anaesthetic can be adjusted as necessary. Precise monitoring means that much smaller doses of anaesthetic can be used than was previously possible.

Microsurgery

Until recently, surgery was limited by the surgeon's ability to manipulate instruments using the naked eye and his or her own hands. The development of microsurgery has enabled surgeons to carry out far more delicate procedures than was previously possible. In microsurgery, tiny instruments are manipulated with the help of a microscope or magnifying camera and often with the assistance of computers or robots. Using microsurgery, severed blood vessels can be reattached and nerves reconnected so that transplanted organs or limbs can function as normally as possible. Operations on the inside of the eye and the inner ear are also possible using microsurgery tools and techniques.

CUTTING EDGE MOMENTS

Landmarks in microsurgery

1921	Carl Olof Nylen (Sweden) first uses a microscope in surgery, to perform delicate operations on the ear.
1922	Gunnar Holmgren (Sweden) invents the binocular operating microscope.
1950s	Julius Jacobson and Ernesto Suarez (USA) develop the operating microscope to repair small blood vessels.
1960s	Bernard O'Brien (Australia) pioneers microsurgical techniques, particularly on the attachment and regeneration of bone.
1965	Susumi Tamai (Japan) carries out the first reattachment of a completely severed finger.
1968	John Cobbett (UK) transplants a big toe to replace a lost thumb.
1985	First use of robotically controlled tools in microsurgery.
2005	First face transplant carried out in Lyon, France.

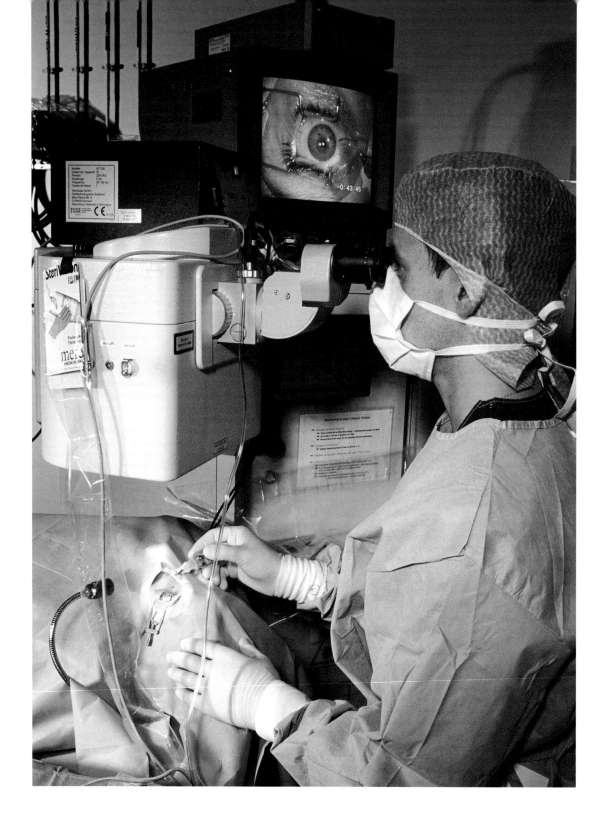

Surgeons operate while looking through a microscope or while using a camera that projects a magnified image of the area being operated on onto a computer screen. The microscopes used for

A surgeon performs laser eye surgery with the help of a microscope connected to a computer.

microsurgery are binocular – they have two eyepieces – which makes it easier for the surgeon to judge distances in three dimensions. Some have two pairs of eyepieces so that two surgeons can look at the operating site at the same time. Surgeons use scaled-down surgical tools to carry out delicate operations. Procedures that can be carried out in this way include making many small joins to reconnect severed or torn blood vessels, nerves, tendons or muscle fibres. During these operations, surgeons often need to make minute sutures (stitches). These are made with nylon or polypropylene only 20 microns thick (a micron is one thousandth of a millimetre) and with a needle that is 50 to 130 microns in diameter. Clamps are available to seal blood vessels with a diameter of less than half a millimetre, and forceps may have tips of only a tenth of a millimetre.

CUTTING EDGE   SCIENCE

Laser eye surgery

Lasers are used widely in eye surgery, both for reattaching the retina (the inside coating of the eye) when it has become detached and to remodel the cornea (the clear membrane over the eye) to correct vision defects. Laser eye surgery, called LASIK, was first carried out in 1990 by Lucio Buratto of Italy and Ioannis Pallikaris from Greece.

Before the operation, a map of the patient's cornea is created using low-power lasers. The patient is given anaesthetic eye drops and a sedative before the procedure, but remains awake. The first stage is to release a flap of the top surface of the cornea with a laser, and to fold this back. The second stage involves using a different type of laser to remodel the lower layer of the cornea, the stroma. The laser vaporizes targeted tissue by destroying the bonds within the molecules. When enough of the stroma has been removed, the flap is folded back over it. The eye heals naturally over the following months.

Lasers

Lasers are high-powered beams of light. They are intensely focused and very narrow, so they can be precisely targeted. A laser can produce very high temperatures, but cool lasers used in surgery are directed at a very small area and do not heat nearby tissue.

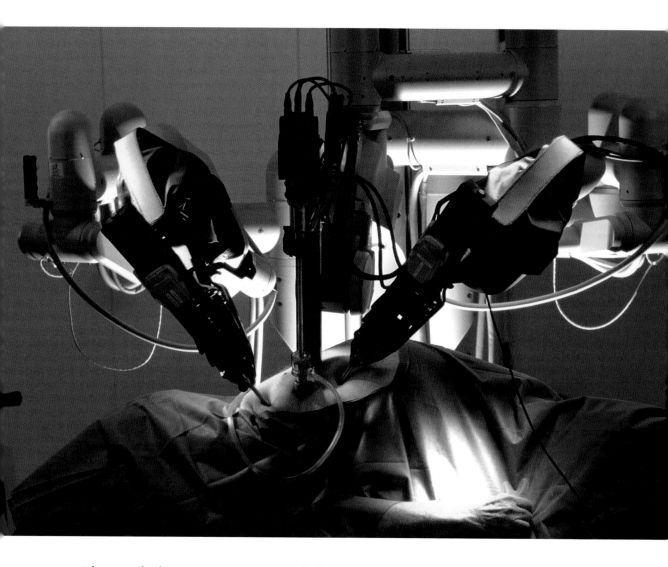

A laser scalpel cuts – or, more accurately, burns – through tissue without causing the damage to adjoining tissue that occurs when a conventional scalpel (surgical knife) is used. It automatically cauterizes (seals) the wound it creates, stopping any bleeding by heat-sealing the ends of blood vessels. Lasers can be used to stop the bleeding caused by a peptic ulcer (damage to the lining of the intestine).

Lasers can be used to destroy tissue, such as cancerous growths, and to cut through bone. Lasers can also be used as a replacement for mechanical drills in dentistry. Coloured tissue (tissue, for example, that contains a lot of blood) is particularly sensitive to lasers, so they can be used to destroy coloured carcinomas

The da Vinci medical robot performs an operation on a patient's heart, working through an incision (cut) only 1 cm long. The surgeon can observe the operation by watching images captured by a camera on one of the robotic arms, and controls the other tools remotely.

(cancerous growths) and destroy the pigment in tattoos, removing the tattoo.

Robots in surgery

In physical tasks, robots can often perform better than a human being. They do not get tired, they do not suffer from tremors or slips, they can make very small and precise movements, and they are not limited by the size of the human hand. Robots are increasingly used in surgery to manipulate tiny instruments in very small spaces inside the body. The expertise of the surgeon is still needed to direct the tools – robotic surgery is an extension of human skill, not a replacement for it.

Robots may be passive or active. A passive robot is used to line up and position equipment, but then a human surgeon carries out the surgical procedure. An active robot carries out surgical procedures. Active robots are already commonly used in joint replacement surgery and to destroy stones or cancerous growths from within the body.

CUTTING EDGE MOMENTS

Robotics and telesurgery

1985	The first use of a robot, the PUMA 560, to place a needle for a brain biopsy, at Memorial Hospital, Los Angeles, USA.
1988	The first human surgery to be carried out by robot, using the 'Probot' at Imperial College, London, UK, on a patient with prostate cancer.
1992	Integrated Surgical Systems, based in Davis, California, USA, develop the ROBODOC to remove bone ready for a hip replacement operation.
1997	Approval by the US Food and Drug Administration of the da Vinci Surgical System as the first assisting surgical robot. It was manufactured by Intuitive Surgical Inc., based in Sunnyvale, California, USA.
1998	The first robotic surgery is performed at the Broussais Hospital in Paris, France.
2001	The first transatlantic telesurgery: a surgeon in New York City, USA, removes the gall bladder of a patient in Strasbourg, France.

Long-distance surgery

The combination of robotically controlled tools and fast computer networks mean that a surgeon no longer needs to be physically present to carry out surgery. A camera connected to a computer can send a live video feed from the microscope to a distant surgeon who can then instruct helpers and control robotic tools. The surgeon may use controls that copy the sensation of actually carrying out the operation – so if there is pressure on a blade because he is pushing against bone, for example, that is mimicked in the robotic controls. The remote use of robots for surgery is called telesurgery. It is particularly useful when an emergency situation arises somewhere that a doctor cannot easily attend, such as on an oil rig, a ship or even a spacecraft – a group in Canada is

A heart-lung machine (in the foreground) is being used to pump and oxygenate a patient's blood during heart bypass surgery.

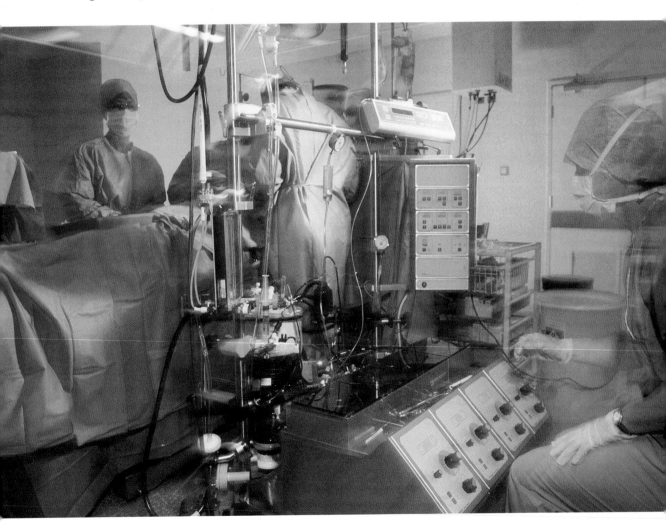

experimenting with carrying out telesurgery techniques in a mock spacecraft, underwater. Telesurgery is still in its infancy, but is developing rapidly.

CUTTING EDGE — SCIENTISTS

John Heysham Gibbon

John Gibbon (1903–1973) was born in Philadelphia, Pennsylvania, USA, into a family of doctors. He trained at Princeton University, New Jersey, in 1923 and at Jefferson Medical College in Philadelphia, qualifying as a doctor in 1927. Upset by the death of a young patient in 1931, Gibbon resolved to find a way of bypassing the heart and lungs to make surgery on the heart possible. Despite the discouragement of colleagues, he experimented independently, succeeding in 1935 in keeping a cat alive for 26 minutes with a prototype heart-lung machine. After World War II (1939–1945), he continued working on his invention with financial support from IBM and produced a machine that worked well with dogs. The first human patient was Cecelia Bavolek who, in 1953, underwent successful open-heart bypass surgery, with Gibbon's heart-lung machine treating her blood. His design was refined at the Mayo clinic in Rochester, Minnesota, and a commercial version, the Mayo-Gibbon heart-lung machine, was produced in 1955.

Heart-lung machines

The heart is one of the most important organs in the body. Without the heart pumping the blood, the brain and other organs would be quickly starved of oxygen, causing damage and then death. In order to operate on the heart, it must first be stopped. This is made possible by a heart-lung machine, which bypasses the heart and lungs, adding oxygen to the blood and pumping it artificially through the patient's body.

The patient is connected to the heart-lung machine and the heart is stopped by cooling it or by the action of drugs. The blood is oxygenated by the machine and returned to the body. Up to 5 litres (1.3 gallons) is removed from the body, treated and replaced each minute. A patient can be connected to the machine for several hours, but the time is limited because eventually the blood is damaged by the process.

CHAPTER 5

Treating Disease

Modern technology offers many possibilities for making the treatment of disease easier and more comfortable for the patient. Treatments range from minor surgical procedures to life-saving operations and the implantation of devices in the body to keep it working properly.

Helping the heart

Heart disease is one of the main causes of death in the developed world. There are many machines that can help the heart with its work, keeping it beating regularly and replacing parts that are damaged.

An artificial pacemaker is a small device implanted in the chest to regulate the heartbeat. It takes over the role of pacemaking cells, a group of cells in the heart, which usually perform this task. If the

CUTTING EDGE   SCIENCE

Pacemaker statistics

- Heart failure affects about 5 million Americans.
- Heart failure costs the USA around $40 billion a year and accounts for 5 to 10 per cent of hospital admissions and 6.5 million hospital days per year.
- Between 1990 and 2002, 2.25 million pacemakers were fitted to patients in the US.
- 17,323 pacemakers were removed in the same period because of faults, half because of battery or capacitor failure. The failure rate is 0.68%.
- 66 patients died because of malfunctioning pacemakers.

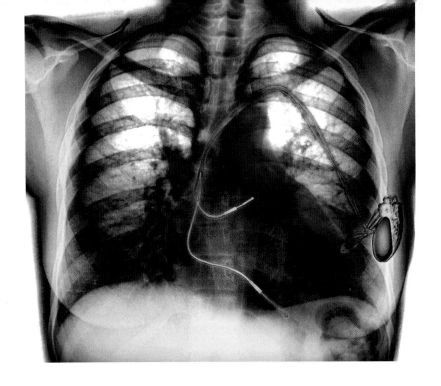

A pacemaker (blue) implanted in a patient's body is revealed by X-ray. The pacemaker is not implanted in the chest cavity, but just under the skin.

cells are destroyed or damaged by disease, or stop working well in old age, they may produce an irregular heartbeat. An artificial pacemaker can replace the cells' function and keep the patient alive for many years. Wires from the artificial pacemaker carry electrical impulses to the heart muscles to make them contract, causing the heart to beat. Pacemakers use lithium batteries that last around seven years and are then replaced in a minor operation.

Early pacemakers were cumbersome external machines, connected to the patient with wires. The first pacemaker to be implanted in a human patient was designed in 1958 by Rune Elmqvist of Sweden. Early models weighed around 180 grams. Today, pacemakers weigh only about 30 grams.

The earliest pacemakers controlled the heart all the time, taking over from the heart's own pacemaking cells completely. Demand pacemakers have been in use since the mid-1960s. These only take over when necessary – when the heart is beating too slowly or too quickly. Since the 1970s, programmable pacemakers have been available. Their settings can be adjusted without surgery, by radio control. From the mid-1980s, pacemakers have been able to respond to the body's need for an increased or decreased heart rate, depending on the state of activity. More recent models 'learn' the patient's own pattern of heart activity under different conditions and adjust to mimic it. They can also record the patient's condition over time and download the information at a check-up.

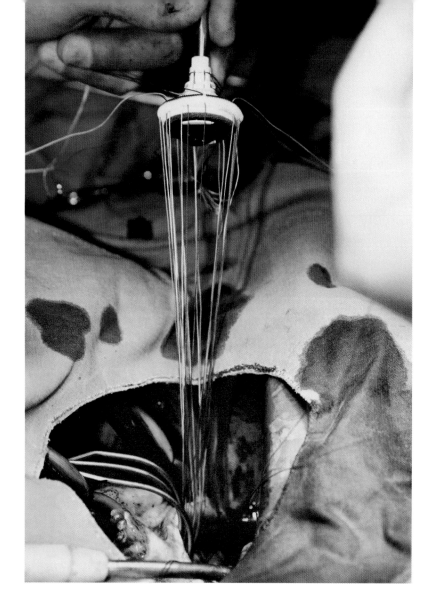

An artificial heart valve is attached to the heart, ready to be pulled into place and secured. The valve is sewn into the heart.

A new Biotronik pacemaker, developed in 2004, communicates by wireless network with a healthcare provider, sending information on a patient's condition. Patients don't need to attend a clinic for check-ups and can live a more normal life – and medical staff are alerted immediately if there are any problems. Soon, transplanted pacemaker cells may be able to restore the natural pacemaking function of the heart without mechanical aids.

Replacement valves

Some heart problems are caused by faulty valves in the heart. The valves make sure the blood flows in the right direction – a valve is like a gate that is kept open by the flow of blood in one direction, but blood pushing on it from the other direction will only close it. Faulty,

CUTTING EDGE MOMENTS

Heart valve history

1952	Charles Hufnagel (USA) develops the first mechanical valve for the heart. Used in the aorta, it is a ball valve that moves up and down in a metal cage with the pressure of blood behind it.
1960	Albert Starr (USA) performs the first successful replacement of the mitral valve (the valve between the left ventricle and left atrium), using a design developed with the engineer Lowell Edwards. The Starr-Edwards valve was made from a steel cage enclosing a silicone rubber ball.
1969	The Bjork-Shiley tilting disk valve is introduced after a high mortality rate is noticed among patients with a narrow aorta, who received ball valves.
1979	The first bileaflet valve, the St Jude Medical valve, is developed. It has two semicircular flaps called leaflets that rotate around struts, and mimics a real valve more closely than a tilting disk or ball valve.

weakened or damaged valves can be replaced by artificial valves.

There are two types of mechanical heart valve. One operates like a door, in much the same way as the original valve, opening in the right direction when the pressure is great enough. The other is a ball valve, with a ball sealing the passage until increased blood pressure forces it out of the way. Both are fixed into the heart during open-heart surgery. The valves work indefinitely and never need replacing, but patients need to take blood-thinning drugs for life to avoid the danger of blood clotting and blocking the valve.

Biological heart valves are also of two types. They may be taken intact from the heart of another animal – usually a pig – and fixed in place in the human heart. Or they may be made on a metal frame from tissue taken from a horse or cow. Complete valves from another animal can lead to rejection problems as the body's immune system recognizes the valve as 'foreign' and fights it. Anti-rejection drugs can help to combat this response. Rejection is not a problem with valves made on a metal frame from tissue. Patients do not need blood-thinning drugs with biological valves, but the valves may wear out after around 15 years and need replacing.

Scientists hope to improve on existing valves in the future by growing tissue over a matrix (the material in tissue that is not composed of cells but provides a structural framework) to make a biological replacement valve. The best tissue to use would be from the patient's own heart, to avoid any risk of rejection.

Artificial hearts

Sometimes, serious heart disease or damage caused by blockages makes the heart unable to function properly. An artificial heart may then be able to take over the function of the heart. At the moment, an artificial heart is only a temporary solution that may be used while a patient waits for a healthy, real heart to become available for a transplant.

An artificial heart replaces the two ventricles – the lower chambers of the heart – with two mechanical pumps. These pump blood into the upper two chambers of the heart, called the atria (which are left in place). The artificial heart is made of plastic, aluminium and polyester and is powered by an external battery. A system of compressed air hoses enters the heart through the chest to operate the pumping mechanism. This means there is a risk of infection, and the equipment involved is cumbersome, so currently artificial hearts are not a long-term solution to heart disease.

Of the two lower chambers of the heart, the left ventricle is the more powerful pump, as it must pump blood out to the rest of the

CUTTING EDGE   MOMENTS

Artificial hearts

In 1957, Willem Kolff, a Dutch-born scientist working in the USA, tested an artificial heart in animals to identify problems. In 1969, a team led by Denton Cooley at St Luke's Episcopal Hospital, Houston, Texas, USA, successfully implanted an artificial heart in a patient who lived with it for more than 60 hours. One of the best-known artificial hearts, the Jarvik 7, was developed during the late 1970s by an American surgeon called Robert Jarvik. The Jarvik 7 was successfully used in patients from the early 1980s. In 1982, a patient lived for 112 days with a Jarvik 7 heart. In 1985, a Jarvik 7 was used to keep a patient alive for a week before he had a heart transplant.

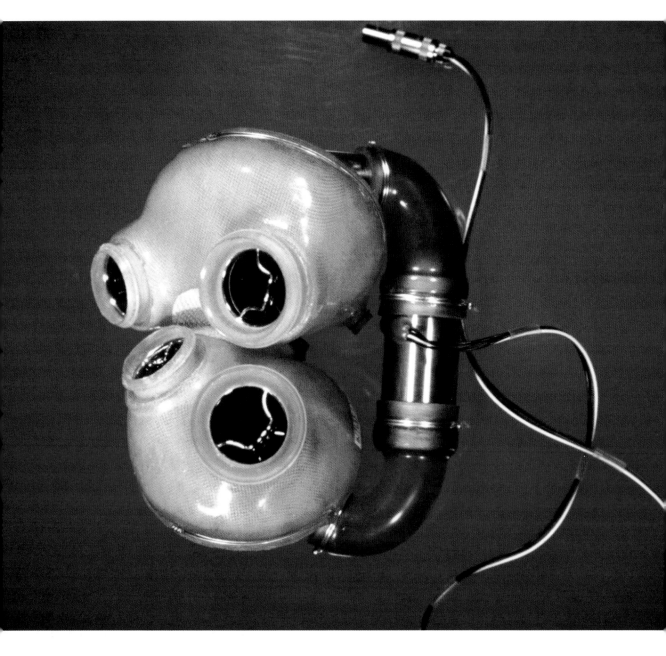

body. When the heart is diseased, the left ventricle is often not strong enough to carry out its work properly, and the patient needs a new heart. While the patient waits for a healthy heart to become available for transplant, he or she may have a machine implanted in the heart to help the left ventricle. This is called a left ventricle assist device (LVAD). An LVAD boosts the functioning of the left ventricle – it is does not take over from it completely.

A Jarvik 7 artificial heart made of aluminium and plastic. The Jarvik 7 was used in the first implant operation in 1982.

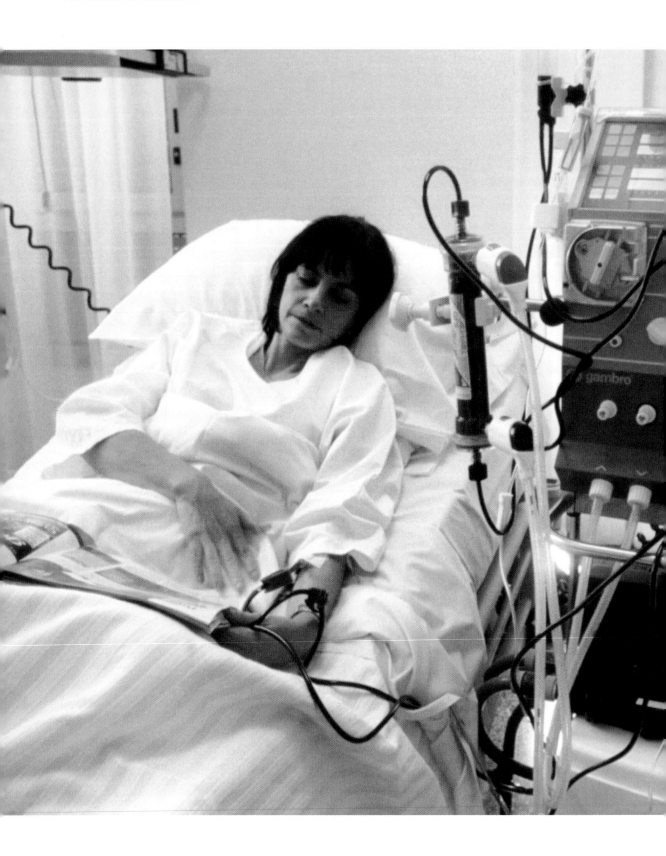

An LVAD draws blood from the left ventricle through a tube to a pump that then sends it into the aorta. The pump is implanted in the upper part of the patient's abdomen. The pump is connected through the wall of the abdomen to an external battery and control system. LVADs are small enough to carry around, so a patient has an acceptable standard of living while waiting for a heart transplant.

The latest LVADs can be used over an extended period, even replacing heart surgery as a method of treatment. They can be used when a transplanted heart is rejected, and to allow a weakened heart time to strengthen and regain its function.

Some LVADs intended for permanent use have the pump as well as the battery outside the body, and are connected to the heart by a tube, which enters the body at the groin.

Kidney problems

The kidneys maintain the water balance of the body and remove waste products, making urine. Failure of the kidneys (renal failure) due to damage or disease can be fatal. In modern medicine, machines can take over the function of the kidneys until they recover or until a kidney for transplant is found. In a process called dialysis, an artificial kidney machine (also known as a dialysis machine, or dialyzer) removes waste from the blood outside the patient's body, before returning the cleaned blood to the body through a vein in the patient's arm.

CUTTING EDGE   SCIENCE

Kidney dialysis
A tube carries blood from an artery in the patient's forearm into a dialysis machine where it passes over a thin membrane (a very thin sheet of porous material). On the other side of the membrane is a reservoir of a sterile solution. Impurities in the blood pass through the membrane, but blood cells are too large to pass through. Before re-entering the body through a vein in the forearm, the blood passes through a trap to remove clots and bubbles. The membranes used in dialysis machines were originally made from animal tissue, but now a layer of hollow cellophane fibres is used.

Opposite: A patient undergoing kidney dialysis, connected to a dialysis machine.

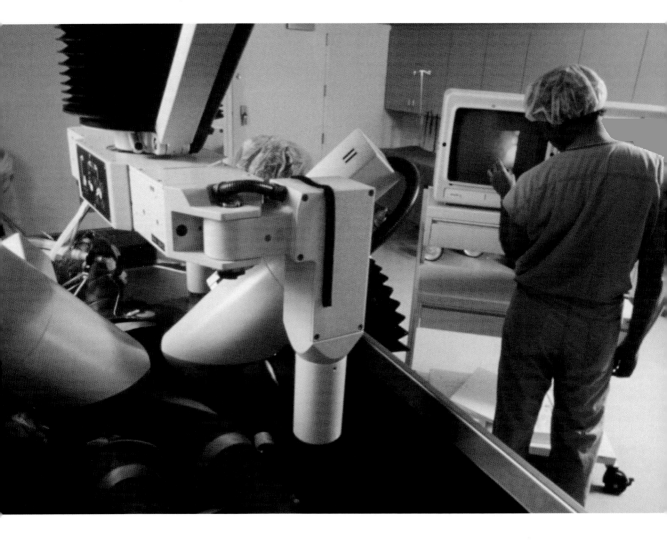

The patient has to be connected to the dialysis machine, either at hospital or sometimes at home, several times a week for around three hours at a time. About 100 million dialysis treatments take place each year around the world.

Kidney dialysis was first tried on animals in 1913 and on a human patient in 1924, but the first practical dialyzer was produced by Dutchmen Willem Kolff and Henrick Berk in 1943. They used a drum with 30 to 40 metres of cellophane tubing wrapped around it, which rotated in a 100-litre tank of dialyzing solution. Although the principle worked, the need to puncture an artery and vein each time meant that a limited number of dialysis treatments could be carried out on each patient. Dialysis became a long-term solution only with the invention of the shunt in 1960 by Belding Scribner

During lithotripsy treatment to break up kidney stones, the patient may be submerged in a bath of water, as water transmits the sound waves well.

46

and Wayne Quinton from the USA. This was a U-shaped tube made of the non-stick material Teflon and connected permanently to an artery and vein in the patient's arm. The dialyser could be plugged into the shunt repeatedly without damaging the blood vessels, and between treatments the tube simply feeds blood from the artery to the vein. This type of shunt is still used today, though made from a different material.

Smashing stones

Sometimes, chemicals build up into hard lumps called stones in the kidney, bladder or gall bladder. These can be very painful and must be removed. As an alternative to surgery, they can be blasted apart using ultrasound or an electrical current. This process is known as lithotripsy.

An alternative to lithotripsy using ultrasound is the application of shock waves produced by electricity. A probe is inserted, usually through the urinary tract, to the stone, and the electric current is delivered along it.

Lasers may be used if the stone does not respond to lithotripsy treatment. Because the laser must be delivered directly to the stone to avoid damaging other tissues, the doctor inserts an endoscope (a thin, flexible tube) into the urinary tract up to the location of the stone in the bladder. If the stone is in the kidney, it is reached through a small incision in the patient's back.

CUTTING EDGE SCIENCE

Sound treatment

Ultrasound is a very high pitched sound that cannot be heard by the human ear. Like all sound, it is transmitted as vibrations through the air and through solid matter. It can be used with a lithotripter to break up stones. A lithotripter is a device that focuses ultrasound waves on the stone with the help of X-ray guidance while the patient sits in a tub of water. The stone breaks up and is passed out of the body in the patient's urine.

Focussed ultrasound can also be used to treat some kinds of cancer and Parkinson's disease (a nervous disorder), and to relieve joint pain as it can heat up specially targeted areas without affecting other parts of the body.

CHAPTER 6

Quality of Life

Not all diseases and damage can be cured, even with the huge advances in medical science and technology made over recent decades. When doctors cannot cure a patient, they try to give them as good a quality of life as possible, providing medicines and devices that help them to live with their condition as comfortably and as independently as they can.

Mechanical joints

As people get older, their joints often deteriorate. The combination of years of use, the gradual loss of elasticity in the body tissues, and

CUTTING EDGE MOMENTS

New hips for old

The earliest recorded attempt at a hip replacement was in 1891 in Germany, using ivory to replace the top of the femur (thigh bone). Steel or chrome replacement joints became widely used in the 1930s, but truly successful hip replacement began with John Charnley's work at the Manchester Royal Infirmary, UK, in the early 1960s. He developed the combination of a metal bone shaft and ball with a socket lined with plastic. His pioneering technique and design have been used ever since, with only slight refinement and changes of material.

The surgeon cuts away the bone of the socket in the hip and the ball shape at the top of the thigh bone and replaces these with metal substitutes. The cup of the socket is lined with polyethylene (a plastic) so that the joint moves smoothly, without friction. The joint may be cemented in place, or its position may be fixed through natural bone growth – that is, new bone will grow to fill the gaps left by surgery.

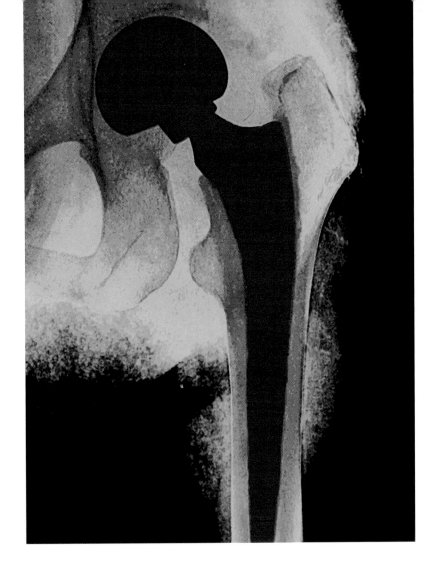

An X-ray of an artificial hip that has been used to replace a diseased or damaged hip joint. The metal of the implant extends down into the femur (thigh bone).

the build up mineral deposits at the surfaces of the bones contribute to conditions that make the joints stiff and painful. Osteoarthritis, a disease in which the bone and cartilage wear away, is particularly common in older people. Many joints, including hip, shoulder, elbow, knee and knuckle, can now be replaced with artificial versions.

Replacement joints copy the shape and mechanics of the original. Materials for joints must be strong, durable, resistant to wear and tear and stable when inside the body. Early models made of stainless steel corroded to some degree. Modern replacement joints are made from alloys (mixtures) of other metals, including molybdenum and titanium used with polyethylene. Recently, some surgeons have used bone resurfacing instead of replacement, removing the surface of the joint and using a polyethylene coating to restore smooth working.

New limbs

If a patient loses a limb through an accident or disease, or is born with a limb missing, a prosthetic (replacement) limb can often give him or her much of the capability of a real limb.

People have been using primitive artificial limbs for thousands of years. The earliest were simple wooden props to replace missing legs, or hooks to restore the most basic use of a hand. Modern artificial limbs look highly realistic, being made of plastics that are carefully matched to the patient's skin colour and limb shape. They also reproduce much of the functionality of the original limb. The latest prosthetic limbs have electronic sensors that can detect nerve impulses in the muscle to which they are attached. Microprocessors process the signals to control the limb, so the person can move it in the same way as he or she would move a real limb.

Artificial limbs are becoming increasingly realistic and sophisticated. The Dextra artificial hand has computer-driven mechanical fingers connected to the user's existing nerve pathways so that they can be controlled just like real fingers. There are pressure sensors in the fingertips so that the user can adjust his or her grip to hold even delicate objects. Scientists are even working on limbs that can be controlled by thought, picking up impulses directly from the brain.

CUTTING EDGE SCIENCE

Cochlear implants

People who are completely deaf may have a cochlear implant – a small device fitted behind the ear and partly inside the head. It provides a way of understanding sound that is not quite the same as hearing – a noise 'heard' with an implant may not sound the same as one heard in the normal sense. A cochlear implant picks up and processes sound, concentrating on the sounds relating to speech, and then converts the sounds to an electric current. The current is passed directly to the auditory nerve, so that the cochlear implant bypasses the non-functioning ear. The sound processing usually works on the patterns of speech, so that the wearer can understand speech. Often, it works well enough that the person can understand a telephone conversation as well as face-to-face communication.

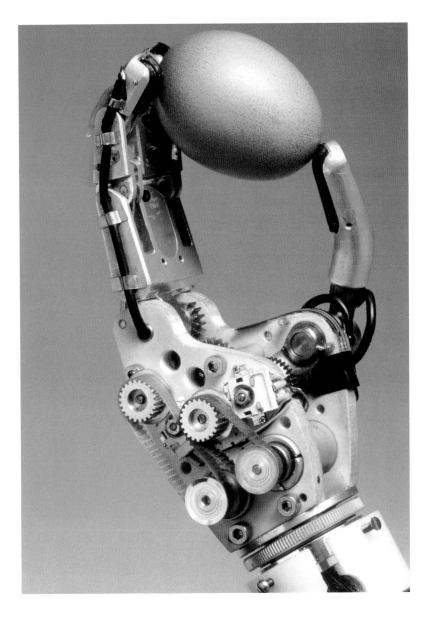

A robotic prosthetic hand is sensitive enough to hold an egg. The batteries in this prototype last only 12 hours, but the design holds out hope for future developments.

Aids to hearing

People who cannot hear well often use a hearing aid to amplify sounds. This sits behind the ear or just inside it, in the outer ear. The hearing aid picks up sounds, which are transmitted as vibrations in the air, and converts them into an electric current. The current is then amplified and converted back into a sound at a louder intensity than the original. A hearing aid can only help someone who has some level of hearing, since it works by magnifying sounds.

Newer, digital hearing aids are more adjustable than older models. They can be set to suit each person's hearing loss and needs, and adjusted to work well in different environments – a noisy football stadium or a quiet library, for instance.

Increasingly sensitive cochlear implants (see panel on page 50) should soon enable deaf people to enjoy music. The new style of implant has four elements that vibrate in response to sound. Each responds at a different, narrow range of frequencies. As it vibrates, it produces a tiny electrical current, which is passed to the auditory nerve (the nerve that carries sound information to the brain). The

This retinal implant is capable of responding to light and passing an electrical impulse to the optic nerve, simulating vision for blind patients.

elements are coated with a special material, which causes them to produce a small voltage without needing a separate power supply. The new design may be available for use from around 2015.

New sight

While people with vision impairment can often use spectacles or contact lenses to improve their sight, people with complete or partial loss of vision may soon be able to use special spectacles that send visual information to a 3 millimetre-long computerized implant in the eye (see panel).

Taking medicinal drugs

Some patients need to take medical drugs for extended periods, even for their whole lives, in order to keep a condition under control. This is the case with people suffering from diabetes, for example. Diabetes is a condition in which the patient's body does not produce insulin (the chemical that controls the removal of sugars by the blood for the body to use). As a result, the blood sugar level rises, causing dehydration and other side effects. People with diabetes need to take insulin daily, to remain healthy.

Methods of administering drugs easily can make life for such people more comfortable and can remove or reduce the danger of them forgetting to take their medication and suffering ill effects.

CUTTING EDGE — SCIENCE

Bionic eye

Researchers at Stanford University, California, USA, have developed a system comprising special goggles that incorporate a video camera and a computer chip implanted behind the patient's retina. The video camera picks up the image in front of the person's eyes and uses a wireless connection to send it to a computer the size of a wallet. The computer processes the information and sends an image back to the goggles, which reflect the image into the eye. The implant has light-sensitive electric cells that are fired by the image. The chip converts the information to electrical pulses in the same way as cells in the retina, and passes these to cells in the inner retina for transmission to the optical nerve (the nerve that carries information from the eye to the brain). This gives the user some experience of sight.

Some drugs can be delivered by implanting a slow-release capsule in the body, called an implanted drug delivery system (IDDS). The drug is released at a steady rate over months or even years. The use of contraceptive implants in the arm can protect women against pregnancy for three years. The implant is a small, flexible rod that releases hormones at a steady rate. There are different types of IDDS:

Biodegradable and non-biodegradable implants A biodegradable implant slowly breaks down in the body, releasing the drug built into it. A non-biodegradable implant does not break down. Both types release drugs passively at a steady rate.

Pumped implant This uses a tiny, remote-controlled pump to adjust the rate of delivery of a drug. It can be useful to deliver pain relief for example, enabling adjustment of the amount of drugs to suit the patient's needs.

Radiotherapy implants Radiotherapy is a type of cancer treatment that uses radiation to destroy cancerous cells. Radiotherapy

CUTTING EDGE   DEBATES

Who chooses whether to implant?

Some of the best drugs for treating psychotic disorders such as schizophrenia can be delivered by IDDS. This avoids the difficulty of disturbed or distressed patients forgetting to take medication, and releases them and their carers from the burden of ongoing, daily medication. But the issue raises concerns about the rights of patients. Some psychiatric patients are not able to make an informed choice about implants. There is debate about whether it is right to use implants in patients who refuse to take medicines but could become dangerous to themselves or others without medication.

Patients' rights groups argue that implanting devices to release mind-altering drugs gives medical staff unacceptable levels of control over patients and could be used to make life easier for staff as much as to help patients. Without a long track-record to establish the safety of the system, vulnerable patients may be being exposed to risks they have not personally consented to.

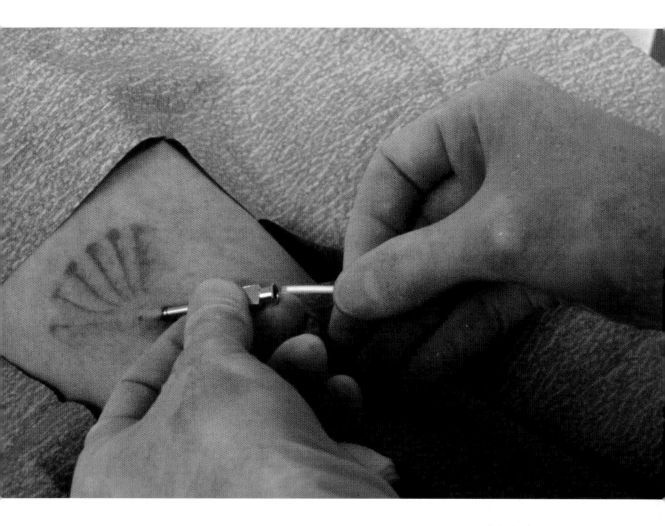

implants can help cancer patients by providing ongoing, targeted medication in the area in which cancerous cells are growing. By treating only the affected area, the unpleasant and damaging side effects caused by exposing large areas of the body to radiotherapy are minimized.

Plastic-coated implants A plastic coating on implants in the heart and arteries often contains drugs that are released steadily. A new design for 'smart' plastic films may soon be able to release different drugs in sequence over a period. Plastic coatings would be added in layers, with drugs sandwiched between barrier layers that are slowly broken down in the body. The coatings would be used on implants such as replacement joints to deliver the drugs needed to optimize the body's acceptance and use of the joint.

A doctor inserts a contraceptive implant under the skin of a woman's arm. Ink marks on the skin show the sites of the implants. The slow release of a hormone will provide contraception for five years.

CHAPTER 7

The Future

The future of medicine will see increasing use of computer technology, and especially of miniaturized systems that can be implanted in the body. Wireless connections make it possible for computers inside the body to be controlled from outside, or to send information to external computers and monitors. Miniaturization will advance, too, with nanotechnology (the art of building microscopic machinery) opening up entirely new avenues of diagnosis and treatment.

Hopes for the heart

Implantable smart chips that monitor the heart, assess its beating rate and pattern, and give early warning of heart attacks, are already emerging. A new implant, the size of a grain of rice, is being developed to measure pressure inside the heart's chambers.

This boy uses a sensor attached to his finger to relay brain impulses to a computer and play a computer game.

The implant has no batteries itself, but is powered by a radio transmitter and receiver waved over it. When triggered by a signal from the transmitter, the implant sends its stored information to the receiver. An implantable chip could save people with fluid build-up in the heart from an unpleasant surgical procedure they would have to undergo several times a year to check the state of their heart.

Thought control

In 2000, a neurobiologist named Miguel Nicolelis, working at Duke University in Durham, North Carolina, USA, trained a monkey to move a robotic arm by thought, using nerve impulses picked up by electrodes implanted in its brain. Researchers at the IDIAP Research Institute in Martigny, Switzerland, are now developing a robotic system that will allow disabled and paralysed people to control wheelchairs or prosthetic limbs just by thinking. The system uses electrical impulses from the brain to relay 'thoughts' to computer technology that controls the devices.

Nanotechnology

Nanotechnology is the science of making very small machinery that can work in tiny spaces, even inside the human body. Nanotechnology works with tiny computer components, so small that they are measured in nanometers (millionths of a millimetre), smaller than a single cell. The aim of many nanotechnology pioneers is to produce devices that will work independently. In medical applications, that may mean that these devices will be able to navigate their way around the inside of the body. Nanotechnology is in its infancy, but its potential applications in medicine are great. Through nanotechnology, it may be possible one day to send microscopic machines into the body to carry out repairs and monitor a person's health.

Computer art image of nanorobots working on brain cells.

A team of researchers at the Chinese Academy of Sciences in Beijing, China, is already working on tiny robots that could be put into blood vessels and 'swim' around, breaking up any blood clots. They would be propelled by a magnetic field applied from outside the body. At 3 millimetres long, the robots are far too large to count as nanotechnology. But as the technology develops, medical researchers hope to be able to build microscopic devices that will navigate their way through the body, fixing problems and constantly monitoring the body's health. These devices could, for example, destroy cancer cells and other harmful structures, or even work inside cells to correct the DNA in faulty genes responsible for inherited disorders. Nano-tools could help to organize or promote the growth and reproduction of cells to encourage healing or regenerate organs, clean up the blood vessels or lungs, and control prosthetic devices.

Computers everywhere

Computers are already widely used in hospitals and clinics. Increasingly, implants and prostheses used by patients will communicate wirelessly with computers to give carers and medical staff instant access to a patient's condition. Machinery used inside the patient's body will become more responsive, monitoring and adjusting to changing conditions and needs.

In addition, computers will play a greater role in the training of medical staff. Several organizations are producing virtual reality systems that allow doctors to experience some of the symptoms their patients endure, including systems that simulate heart disease, several types of blindness, schizophrenia and stroke. The training aids help medical staff to empathize with their patients and better understand their needs and limitations. It is likely that many more virtual reality systems will emerge, both to help doctors understand medical conditions and to train them safely in surgical procedures.

CUTTING EDGE MOMENTS

Nanotubules kill cancer cells

In 2005, researchers at Stanford University, California, USA, discovered that they could destroy cancer cells and leave normal cells unharmed using a combination of nano-scale tubes of carbon, known as nanotubules, and a laser. The nanotubules are only half the width of a DNA molecule, and thousands can fit into a single cell.

Some cancer cells have receptors on their surface for a vitamin called folate, but normal cells do not. Researchers exploited this difference to make sure that only cancerous cells absorbed the tubules. They coated the nanotubules with folate so that only cancer cells could absorb them. In the body, a laser directed at the area of the cancer would then cause the nanotubules of carbon to heat up rapidly, exploding the cells. Normal cells are unaffected by the laser. Tests on tissue in the laboratory show that the system works, but human trials have not yet started.

Glossary

anaemia A condition in which there are too few red blood cells.

anaesthetic A drug which causes a person to lose sensation, so feel no pain. A general anaesthetic puts a person to sleep, and a local anaesthetic numbs an area of the body.

aorta The large blood vessel that carries blood from the left ventricle of the heart to the rest of the body.

artery A thick-walled blood vessel that carries blood from the heart to the body or lungs.

atria (plural of atrium) The two upper chambers of the heart.

bacteria (plural of bacterium) Micro-organisms present in soil, air and water, which often cause disease.

cancerous growth An abnormal growth in the body caused by cancer. Cancer is an illness in which a group or groups of cells begin to grow uncontrollably.

cardiologist A medical specialist on the heart and blood circulation.

carpal tunnel syndrome A condition in which a nerve in the wrist is compressed, compromising use of the hand or causing painful or uncomfortable sensations.

chromosome One of 23 long structures in the cell nucleus of humans. Each chromosome is a single DNA molecule.

cornea The transparent layer covering the front of the eyeball.

diabetes A condition in which the body cannot produce insulin (the hormone that controls blood sugar levels) or does not respond properly to it, causing excess sugar in the blood.

diagnosis Working out what is wrong with a patient.

dialyzer A machine used for dialysis.

dialysis The process of cleansing the blood of impurities artificially, replacing the function of the kidneys.

DNA A complex protein from which chromosomes are built, encoding the genetic make-up of an organism.

embryo The early stage of development of an unborn baby, from the time when the fertilized egg has started dividing until eight weeks after fertilization.

enzyme A protein found in living things, which speeds up the chemical reactions that are essential to life.

epidemic A widespread and rapidly spreading outbreak of an infectious disease.

epilepsy A disorder of the nervous system causing periodic loss of consciousness.

forceps A medical tool rather like scissors or tongs, used for holding or pulling.

gene A fraction of a chromosome that has the genetic coding for a single characteristic.

heart attack A serious condition in which insufficient blood supplies the heart muscle, usually because of interrupted blood flow.

heart-lung machine A machine that replaces the function of the heart and lungs during an operation, oxygenating and pumping the blood.

immune system The body's defence against disease – it fights and destroys cells it does not recognize as belonging to the body.

incubator A special crib for caring for newborn babies in which temperature and atmosphere can be controlled.

insulin A hormone produced by the pancreas that controls the level of sugar in the blood.

laser A powerful, precisely focused beam of light.

leukaemia Cancer of the blood cells.

matrix A part of tissue that is not composed of cells, but provides the structural framework.

membrane A very fine layer of tissue.

muscular dystrophy A group of disorders causing progressive muscle weakness and wastage.

nanotechnology Technology that uses components on a microscopic scale, measured in nanometres (a millionth of a millimetre).

nanotubules Very tiny cylinders of carbon, a few nanometres in diameter (a nanometre is a millionth of a millimetre).

neonatal Relating to newborn babies.

nerves Bundles of cells that carry messages to, from and within the brain as electrical impulses.

nervous system The system of nerves, spine and brain that carries and processes information coming into the body and gives instructions to move the body, including controlling involuntary actions such as digestion, breathing and temperature regulation.

neurobiologist A person who specializes in the study of how nervous systems work in humans or other animals.

nuclei (plural of nucleus) The centre of a cell, where most of the cell's activity and control is carried out.

osteoarthritis A disease caused by the breakdown of cartilage in the joints, resulting in stiffness and pain.

pacemaker A device implanted under the skin, which transmits electrical pulses through a wire inserted in the heart to regulate the heartbeat.

polio A serious infection that can cause permanent paralysis.

prosthetic Relating to an artificial replacement for a body part.

protein A substance that makes up living structures such as skin, hair and muscle and also controls processes inside cells.

psychiatric Relating to mental illness.

psychotic Relating to mental illness that makes people believe things that are not real.

rejection The body's immune system fighting against implanted tissue.

respirometer A device designed to measure the rate of respiration (breathing).

retina The inside surface of the back of the eye, with light-receptive cells.

schizophrenia A serious mental illness in which a person cannot distinguish between the real and the imaginary.

sepsis A bacterial infection of the blood.

side effects Unwanted effects of a drug or other treatment.

smear test The removal of a few cells from the cervix (neck of the womb) for cancer testing.

stroke A change in blood supply to the brain, which often causes temporary or permanent loss of movement, speech or another ability.

symptom An abnormal sensation or change in bodily function experienced by a patient.

transplant The replacement of a diseased or damaged organ with a healthy one from another person.

ultrasound Waves of very high frequency sound.

ventilator A machine to assist breathing.

ventricle One of the two lower chambers of the heart.

vital signs Signs that show a person's state of health. They include breathing, heart beat, blood pressure and temperature.

Further Information

BOOKS

The Cutting Edge: Medicine by Anne Rooney (Heinemann, 2005)

Lasers by Nina Morgan (Hodder Wayland, 1996)

Medicine Now by Anne Rooney (Chrysalis, 2003)

Scalpels, Stitches and Scars: A History of Surgery by John Townsend (Raintree, 2005)

Technology All Around Us: Medicine by Kristina Routh (Franklin Watts, 2005)

WEBSITES

www.makingthemodernworld.org.uk/icons_of _invention/medicine/
Inventions of medical machinery since 1750.

www.medicalnewstoday.com/sections/medica l_devices/
News of the latest developments and breakthroughs in medical technology.

www.newscientist.co.uk
Website of the weekly journal *New Scientist*, which carries news of developments in medical technologies and treatments.

www.nhsdirect.nhs.uk/selfhelpguide/
A self-diagnosis site provided by the National Health Service in the UK.

Index

Index <small>*(continued)*</small>